A Several World

A Several World

Brian Blanchfield

Nightboat Books
Brooklyn & Callicoon, New York

© 2014 Brian Blanchfield
All rights reserved
Printed in the United States
Second Printing, 2015

ISBN: 978-1-937658-17-5

Cover image wrap: Dennis Oppenheim.
Wishing the Mountains Madness, 1977.
Four acres covered, near Missoula, Montana.
© Dennis Oppenheim.

Design and typesetting by Margaret Tedesco
Text set in Garamond and Stymie BT

Cataloging-in-publication data is available
from the Library of Congress

Distributed by the University Press of New England
One Court Street
Lebanon, NH 03766
www.upne.com

Nightboat Books
Brooklyn & Callicoon, New York
www.nightboat.org

Contents

Four

A Several World

Eclogue Onto an Idea

Up ahead out here, and his affiliate, rival in the eyes,
        someone near, but not our crowd, someone whom
you approach in a poem only
to the extent of his vantage out, to the verb open out
onto. To that extent, you fit into his
looking suit, to the glove points, othering,
a long parenthesis of lens, a self sort of, a caul kind of
first feeling, to the doubled pocket
mouth. Kissed him from inside:

                        what's yes in any *es gibt*, contributing thus
the plus of a little sentience. Have you too felt extra fleetingly?
The early given is he faces the same way we, as though
we sent him to this promontory. To him assign
yourself, and borrow charge. What part of us
you are yet, and what through him and his would I,
if I were you, retrieve in the purview—or whom,
if you want someone with a look, sending looks,

        someone underway and expressing it, someone
drawing from ceremony sensation, separating her own
from others'—gets lost in happening. This is their scene.
Situation's giving onto someone.
Put out some hedge and overhear.
The foreground and the horizon are idea's.
Consider the milieu durance.
Way out there now.

The City State

Remember in Corinth, walking home from the piers, wet
in the aftermath of a squall? Through the meat packing streets,
under bigger hooks blood slick on the sandals, across

the garment district: bone buttons, stronger cord or—what
more did you need?—hard rolls, then fish and flowers in
descending sectors, aspirin and batteries in your arms

for the apartment. Remember answering machines? The gods,
be they pleased, of whichever specific needs, accommodating
singly. Barnaby, after the tone, *this is the guy from the grove.*

Peaches are in. Snap beans (ping in the bowl). *Good surprises*
if you hike up into the higher coppices with me in mind.
Along the manifold fulfillment of local plans, outlanders

often strode through hollering, singing the uncertain song,
and so we expected we knew the words—any deities
to propitiate, la la—when, in the melody familiar, a man

and a youth drew us to the window. Good news they called up,
delivery. Emissaries broadcasting a smirk, saying what still
from the sill we could only oversee. Remember how soon

we found none of the old options applied. Talk. Listen. Door.
I do this one thing all day long and so do you, I know now, first
Corinthians. I squat on the fire escape for better connection.

Funny Loss of Face

Late in the last of the sun all over the wall
across the lot the bordello larks on the ivy vine
visit one another's resting closets
like boys and men in Taiwanese baths:
anyone could be behind that leaf or must he
prefer sleep to sharing sleep, the overcome one,
flustering, not just anyone, retorts
and have him know, special again only once
the turnkey checks, before the wind top to bottom
as in a movie of itself plays the shuddering
singularity of love, selecting no one
particularly anyway, but all in las peliculas
sit deeper in their popcorn parkas down.
Everyone's in for the night except
you who had flown all day didn't want to fall asleep
here I was telling your neck relax your eyes
were going to wake up raw without solution
for lenses, so it was better you find
the little baths they had at home. Why it was
funny I suggested we concoct it from scratch's hard
to say and whether one of us or which was
good about everything. When you call and
the leaves are brighter red, it's later, nearer
the sun, and relief is that vibrant.
That you can see already where more doors
were and birds the ropey circuitry
the wall will bare is an occupancy of mine.

Paranoia Places Its Faith in Exposure

—Eve Sedgwick, *Touching Feeling*

Some touch is received and the sensation is entire
at contact, and some touch there is a rising into. Lucky
the lover who is encouraged to fit or press
into the hand presented, lucky to have a hand, gloves off.
The hard jar against eyetooth and black jowl the tom
engineers if a fist presents, the kitten in the brick cinders
beneath the broken road, its dusty body knowledgeable.
Pick me up can also be as frequency and antennae do.

According to Herodotus

The Phoenicians were good at trenches. A channel
with steep sides often broke, they saw, so
they knew to widen out near the lip.
If they were digging waterways, about twice as wide
as volume demanded was optimal
for coursing.

With bridges, not so much. Built a couple crossing
a strait, one made of flax, and the other,
papyrus. That is history. A paper bridge
didn't hold, though, after a storm, doesn't. That
is engineering. The final chariot
is the chariot befitting the king, carted right up
to overlook what he had arranged
to surpass. Wouldn't. That is policy.
A people far from sovereign.

Good at trenches, bad at bridges.
On the job after the ransack and pillage
of another people. Only in Arizona and only now
is Phoenician a demonym. I mean, what I heard is
there was no Phoenix home
to Phoenicians destroying Greece
for Persia. Only a story of a bird upstart
where another bird burned. Demonym has its own
Wikipedia page. The word is
twenty-two years old. Imagine your own
twenty-two year old [demonym here] here:

curly hair, lashes, headphones if you like.
Tell him, if you like, learning where he's from,
what he is. Now imagine

learning where he's from, being what you are,
sending him back. That is
statecraft.

Edge of Water, Nimrod Falls, Montana

Bareness in greater proportions, bare
in the pairing, the slow man and his son;
that estimation, too, the boy steps ahead of. Behind,
upshore, a study of the swimming hole and his
buttery way down the rocks, rippling dilemma
who, it will be said, must learn to shave,
whose aptitude on his own pertains. If uncircumcised, sorry
and self-innocent, example. For feet, the wet white dumplings
manage for now the body weight. Then, immersion, then
a shallow paddle he picked up somewhere.

No place is dangerous. The situation arrives
as we do. *Dad*, when he wants someone
to give attention; *Butthole*, he calls back to the bank
to chide what he contrives is caution, when
contrivance suffices; *Baby*. The man stands dry.
The boy remarks the cooler water in the cove.

There and back, imitation bats, cliff swallows
hector the falls and the sulfur air and recur
to the limestone, a thousand-chambered console.

Starter Garden

In the gravel was planted some grass
in sprigs. Sort of Garamond, ornamental, it
rounded down. Among many variants
commonest he said. He liked having it
pointed out.

From Baja Barbara wrote the sitter to say
send me an image of my house. I forget
how much of me there is in it. Imagine
seeing over your phone into the blue
Pacific.

This brick, same as all six tangent
to it, is, like a dead tooth, nemesis.
Play with me. Pretend antipathy
and make ground against a tension too.

Picture upon the man a papoose
and in the papoose a daughter, now
grown, infant then. How late
this love for men, any one of them
passing.

The arc is gentle, horizon bowed only
a bit, for instance. Now, shower rain
therefrom, hot condensation back
in the bath. You are buoyant, scalded,
pelletted. Assumption all about you.

Plans for a ramada. A busted clumsy
storage door and netting. The sun
came out and earmarked the farther
barrel. None of this reminds me of
heterosexuality.

Which of These Alberts

Erstwhile Albert

The toss of dress is something by which to infer
a man stands there to catch and sort. A man
who knows the regalia well, who is met
sooner than the air conditioning
at his folding table, who has himself
worn the circle and stripe, number and strap
and goggle. A former albert
who will not shrink from the onrush of handsomes
makes like surrender however
the handover of silks and plunges them under suds.
The plug-faced heckuva and they exude what
compact alberts have across the years.
Not much on the bulletin board
of his face, but his notice is a certain sign.

We, most of us glassed in the sanctum,
remark impunities alberts have,
and to estimate is natural at the glass;
by remarks we make ourselves proportionate.
The toss is youth, surrender age.
An erstwhile albert is not available
for boot pull. Here we come in to squire.

White Albert

Second nature when an albert mounts a stool
and stands a little in his seat, whose stockings report

the floor is spotless, a point of pride. When Albert
mounts a stool in his stockings either
to have himself groomed or to maneuver through
provided diversion, another
player stands behind and sympathizes
with his body, or off to the side. He, irreducible, too,
in his whites, sleeveless and easy: a fullness
in the carriage. At the inmost chamber
you have your work to do, and he his,
and the shaven cheek and the whites you wear
are albert and squire together work.

What does Albert need dampened and draped,
and where. What is fabric Albert wants his
fetlock bandaged by. Say your mentee says:
counsel's standard clause. I doubt anyone's
knees were more ruined than mine, back there
a claret blare away from recovering
my numbers. Albert, are you coming?

Layabout Albert

Ecco Homo on the courtesy billet, but
what he reads is magazines. Among men
an Adonais, and albert-trained, the albert takes
the downtime serious. At the monitors
he sells an interest in infield preparations,

a devotee however to his own

retreat upstage, breaking clearance to castle king

and rook. In the rivalry we ride hard

we give the basket our albert shells and switch

to him allegiant squires. Break then the yet.

The squire I emulate wraps his albert in

a service towel. I don't know when

I've seen the sun. And then his own bare arm

idly withdraws its idle support of Albert's

even jaw, a notice opportunity passed over,

and that's my job, right up to tournament time,

to finish his round on double bended knee,

to read an albert billying, to count

him off and log it in, to work more

the note on methodology.

Gadabout

for SR & KB

A strawberry on the lawn
A Tuesday
       the tortoise goes inside or comes out

       always   either   twice

A Tuesday strawberry on the little lawn
a man has mown

         Another man enjoys
the study of what she'll do
              (what she does she first undertakes to do)
as presentation of data, or so the suitor lays the finding out

Habitat comes by habit, a home by homing in.

Sometimes she takes it,
            and it's won't not can't if she doesn't.

Not always Tuesday. The man cottons to
              deliberateness
     reluctantly.

The cap off   wet from the sink
            with or without a little song

                    His friend
admires this most about the man,
their closeness sweet and warm, closing
even their eyes in age in one another's
company.

          The tortoise, this frank

                    unprotected penis

     emerges,
               pulls herself to

     the singular fruit.

Nurse Mustn't Rummage

Even then and although a latecomer's look around
suggested I had confused the given with consent
and my keep for comprehensive
I burnished the tunic. It was disintegrating;
I brought it on as once a gloss was brought out.
Even then and however assiduous still I
found my flagrancy and, david of me, divulged.
And, raising myself, soaked lip to chin in compote,
shot back a telling giant glance.
What ordnance tore down,
revealing, eaten hungry,
from the looks of me:
original insufficiency.

If no one grew up of the integer—you
know the one—I raised myself, and was to be a man,
in him grew a throat around the fear, once around,
to feel it rise and a valve to catch
its olive taste
and send it—person to personnel—below.
A bete noir, a weak suit, one that breathes.
Never is it imperiling integrity that
depresses the call button. Nothing so helped me
more. Who may I say is leaving ill enough alone

and what is all this antecedent
pulling moreover on
the fitted bedding of malingerers?

What've I got here before I got here
that isn't—outpatient intake—
there there consolation?

Him I found in the dative case
thrown concussive on the very air, west expectancy:
he said I sat close enough to notice if I wanted
his black eyes burgeon at cruising altitude
and before descent he could, he believed, if I wanted,
taste it rocking back,
like dialing a memory.

Man Roulette

What booth is this? The last was a plastic gallows.
In the teach me to kiss booth, you paid your dollar
to promote, when prompted, a theory. Advised me about
standing close and touching him who might next enter
in such a way that draws contrast, rough and smooth,
cool and warm, maybe the heel of the hand and thumb
at the neck if the collar is open and the fingertips two
three four, but never anything about the mouth, and then
it was time. I back exited through the heavy drapes
and opened shop next door.

What booth is this?
In this booth I have rescued a dovekie but it will not eat.
As the tub fills I need you (tore your ticket, right?)
to surrender two of the goldfish from this bag. I'll be
back in a minute. The last of the sun is pinkening
the ridge beyond the fairgrounds, and I'd like to see.

What booth is this? Keep moving everyone.
Careful of the gourds; they're pursing. I've handed over
the last admission I can afford. Into this booth the branch
of a bean tree descends and in an eventuality
brought on by what yet I cannot say the armlong pods
burst with pellet shot pressure and release seeds like these
embedded in the board behind you. The next booth
is one I have to man for someone. An emergency. I'll
meet you there.

Is this even a booth? In this booth there is
room for one. Get in here and hold me up.
I would fall without you. Why are we not told plainly?
What good as a booth is this, what booth if it be one?
Feel the first drop, as from a shearwater ocean bird held high
for miles on the cyclonic air, blown far inland, never
otherwise seen. The barometer is bottoming. This booth of
ours is an eye of the storm simulation.

Open House

We came in here to pretend. Or, rather, they suffer a run on
faith who predicate their commission on windfall,
and that's us. We saw an opening *in situ*.
The realtor was already inside the document we opened
and encouraged us to roam the levels, helping us
to imagine a family outgrew the rooms. Motivated,
she allowed. On spring days, a wind picking up, homosexuality
blows right into the sale of synthesis, and impresses, as if
we could explain. She entrusted herself exclusively
to the parlor floor, so we could call out, wherever we were
in the square footage, our running queries, like a family,
meanwhile prowling, meanwhile fitting our practices to
the built-ins—concrete slabs and formatting palettes at the wall
and window—meeting eyes in the walk-in until the term *radiant*
heating could flare, following by texture and temperature instinct
dimly understood, onto the balcony and into on-demand
water control panels, a room of them. To return respectively
where Wanda waited for candor going forward. We are two men
who can agree in murmurs there is no purchase
any more in Hart Crane, but we'd keep a room for him
called Eileen Myles. What is it about the pretense we belong here
that requires an agent? Or, is that the trouble, Wanda? To whom
to speak at the bank and about what not yet are we
prepared to say. We blew in notional. Somewhere in here
I once wrote some poems Eileen liked that Nijinsky could send
to his remote beloved and they demanded Diaghilev,
his signatory, the management, misunderstand the love
on tour at hotel intervals, the suite if not the marquee ever

in his name, remember, an imprimatur that effaces. One man,
another, and an other. Stamps his foot. Rigid valences over
the bayview, remember, in the same print as the drapes:
I drew them, then took that down and put it in
storage. Here, against the reclaimed material the builders
appropriated, and other disenfranchised phrases, it makes
a statement. Wanda, we weren't faking exactly. Is it better to say
the cyclone fencing traffics in the paper trash the wind
found overnight or to have the wrappers spirited up against it?
We were merely on a walk we had predicated on commotion,
copyists no less than Bouvard and Pecuchet, no less prudential,
who needed only first to agree to fail in turn at every venture
except lifelong life together. In the follow-up,
I'll need to admit my credit is better off undisturbed.
Apologist, archivist, agent, eminence, front, Wanda
there's no room to call you muse. In the variorum, I had
this idea, upstairs and to the left. After dinner you're welcome
to stay for coffee. Not far from here, strewn broadly,
we found a board game, and the penalty cards were prettiest.
What we do is turn them, escalating the damage
a player'd encounter, as a poem builds, or a bid, until his turns
are mortal, a chill Belle Islander, the thinkable tertium quid.
To reside, to inhabit, to dwell: did you know they're all cognate
with staying? Wanda, together we have six thousand dollars.
Which, if it blew away, you might call *some* six thousand dollars.
Listen, pianissimo, the love of things irreconcilable.
That's not us, not any more. But, we keep a room for it.

Thank You Mood

I rang the doorbell with my voice. I was home.
I forgot that could happen. An occasional hoot.
To find indoors the bell ringing, ringing still, recommender
thereby of bells, answerable man high in his range.
Where can I submit this preference over digital?
This morning, neighbors, my attentions were lifted,
lifted by my spirits. I forgot that could happen.

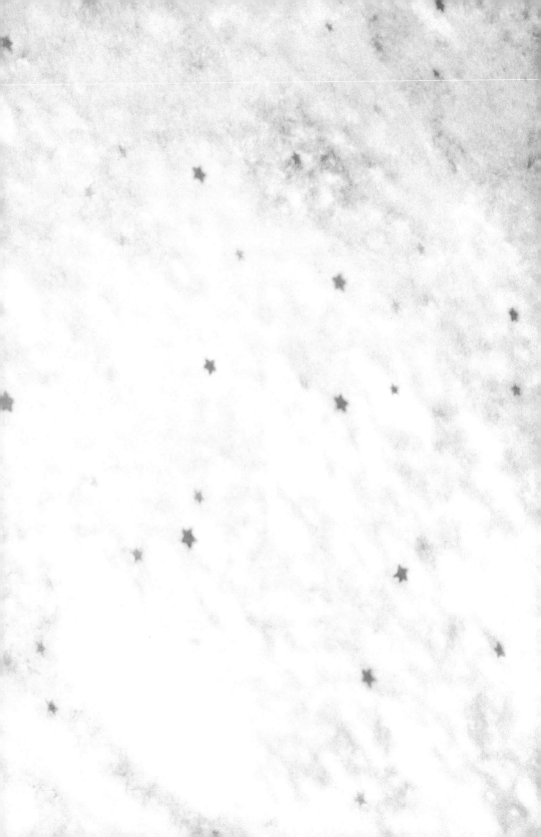

Pferd

Marino Marini, Bechtler Museum of Modern Art

Gift Swiss, holding American, art Italian, tradition
Boeotian. The diabetic buckles on the expo path,
dislodges the fizzy headset and—would it be cavalier
to add—misses in the Snapple retrieved for him

the incidental part Marini plays in the tour of art
a love poem once underwent, beloved incidental, he
on whose behalf from all the world's unconcern
one circulating suitor contrived express concession.

Anyway if there is a homologue in the Frick what
can it mean in Charlotte, stooped at the centerpiece,
in powered-down posterity, in a sugar low,
North Carolina?
              Not rearing, and no rider, right
or wrong, so by the four hooves bronzed
into the tray base no honorific casualty's
inferred; but the stance braces, that is, informs

an agony, an agony then the horse's alone, as though
to throw high and backward the head on the spine
were despair that the slab will slide. Groundless
the figurative foal in full maturity modern, that is,
oblique. What else call it to be cavalier, material,

about the pain of one you bring about to pain?
The controlled spill of more manufacture beneath
inheres in modernism but is, in area, the bed no

more of a boy who climbs into the toy to celebrate
his protracted trample, or to play at spartan sleep,
a mean and final floor to test his cheek for bone.

How often did he wake, the namesake child
whose congeries at angel level benefactors
rebuilt a home, and catch the study Ernst
had made of WC Fields, rotund as a commode,
twirling an umbrella made substantially of rain,
and revolve the pony patrolling spooks.

The hairless body so smooth the risen scoop
of orifice is more singular, ocular, and since
cleanly the spout and dress of tail has been, in
the signature stub above, arrested,
a medallion plumped, from there the line
leads the unrestricted eye beneath the rump to
the retractions of phallus in undercarriage
custody.
           What is it supposed to mean, in Charlotte
or he'll faint and seize, the sweetest, densest
thing you have and hurry, North Carolina? This
would have been just after the war. How again did
O'Hara do away with his Memorial Day 1950?

The stone in uprisen turmoil is the sculptor's
work, but the patina on the flare of nostril
is the touch of the patrons' children who

mounted the petered pony, locked
foursquare on its outspread hocks against
the flat pan of pewter as though it could escape
him, who mounted him and rubbed his
beestung or terror-fixed muzzle green. Did they
say that in your audiotour. I said,
Did they tell you that in your audio tour?

S Apostrophe S

The pelican cocks higher her wing
for good get at. Nibbling the blister
and siphoning the mud by bill to the brood.

Hey, how did the consecration go?

Aristophanes and Judas, but not
Johns. Memphis's (emphasis mine)
on the Mississippi, but not on the Nile.

Hey, how was the peroration?

The bronzer devises a rapprochement,
the mulcher, the parents, the host. She
plans to rephotograph the memorial bench.

So, what was the beseechment like?

Bluing is a way to whiten, the bottle of
bluing agent reads. It takes its place
beside the finish. Or should I have said solution?

Hey, where will you be for Thanksgiving?

Or else I were alone in thinking something
had been in the air, a frost phenomenon,
a pestilence, the AM station's affiliate switch.

But, then, who gave the benediction?

With a tail as big as a kite, for something that
by itself repeats. The windsock on the helipad
and blame enough to go around.

So, what was the turnout in the end?

Two in a pew, one stressed,
the turn down in the thread of her halo
screwy. And whose little boy is he?

Eclogue of Sig Alert on the Ten East

Larry Johnson, The Hammer Museum, Los Angeles

Then the car three back liberated itself from the line
and rolled ahead on the shoulder to the exit.
  And, on this occasion when a car carrying no one you knew
  or thought you knew passed your passenger door, you honked.
I pressed the horn as if involuntarily, a moment longer than desired.
  You were upset?
It was a jealousy honk.
A salute. I saluted the manumission I myself wanted.
  Is that analysis of the behavior or the behavior itself?
I spoke with my father this morning, the one married to my mother.
When you come to a contradiction, make a distinction. That was William James.
  William James quoting someone. Is your father, the other, alive?
Both. On the one hand a car of joyriders maneuvers out of the path
I was forging in the presumption presumably that to move is better
than to proceed.
  Your father called with a matter of significance?
I called him. He has had a medical disappointment, followed by
a health setback. He said of his dire straits not to bother worrying. Then
added, this is the whole ball game.
  Were you at any time pressing him to feel an emotion?
It was like the joyriders were a hustler I could
in a more mobile situation proposition. All the way,
he might say, if rolling my window down I asked—
  How far were you going?
—How far are you going? That, in the walking way of standing still.
  The question is concealed, expressed in that manner.
The turnoff was already in my rearview, by the time I saw
what they had in mind. It may be apparent that I admit nothing
when I write myself such a ticket.

Did your father, either, honk, in the manner you imagine?
The price is written right there under the name of the game.
The name of the game is the names of opponents,
followed by the date and sometimes venue. Free of a charge.
I write them out myself. I might never be rid of these. Free
of a problem.

      A sort of share, an issuance. In that, are you much different than
      every father's daughter?
And then one was way ahead on the highway, son and heir in his hair.
Is there a problem officer? I'd like to speak freely.

By and By

At the end of the meadow riven
in the longest dream by the young lead
kicking the reeds with boots brazenly,
if we are to see his distance by then as a ray
extending still hours over years
we might admire the stage of it.
This is a long shot over the southern canopy
revealing the Clearwater throughway
the beaten path once beaten will meet,
as the boy is yet prohibited to learn. A log
floats at least the distance he has thus far
traveled. The log does little but turn
effortless. His promise to himself is forming
as sycamore ties wet beneath riverside rails
brighten by steps at sundown and
underfoot one is seared with something.
Five or six words. Interdiction feel. In dream
science, they call this signage. In house style
set in small caps. It typically dissipates.
Often a child's start out is Christian
in his hellbent way. The river
turned down and the log went
merrily, if not the boy, to Clearwater,
should he keep on. There is no final tie
transverse to the rails, except the tie
laid overtop. WHY ARE WE NOT TOLD
PLAINLY? The hymns call it homecoming,

tactically, the distance reached
at a grown man's pace. The boots again
have the camera's attention. Cicadas are sent up
hip-high in firework sprites each stride. The sun on
the meadow burns itself off like hay.

Wheelwright & Smith

A wheelwright in the glen trains his young
son on the forge and the while cures his deer
meat at the spring. The water cold and swift
makes it last. Trains his son, that is,

to shape and cool the hitch. A hitch
is anything one carries from spring to hilltop
like a son, or is a hard bulb universal. There are both
meanings. A freight on wheels drags against the trail
but for the wheels. The trail can lead
over passes and dales full of dwellings
providence has had to ditch. Up the old
pigpath a bad deal in the weeds.
The wheelwright raises a smith
after his ampersand,

but the trade card the son enterprises
to distribute among travelers he never
prints until the wheel of the old man's passing parks
and the horse is unyoked. Then empties a sigh
into winter. It took this lifetime to learn
the trench suggesting settlers stay a while
was his doing too, drawing on
far more than the team could manage,
attached to his other idea: up and go
had ever been as popular as abide, & at that rate,
to set out was likewise heritage here.

Fanning across the Blue Ridge and piedmont
dismay and its parent Calvinism
intermarried more, Primitive Baptists and
highwaymen, until: Huguenot in her broad face and hymnal;
rumbling, he, like his brothers atop
the overhead-valve pushrod engine. Age 28 by 1980,
the census records his profession as
tractor trailer dispatch manager. One hitch, 7.

In Their Motions

At an intersection of lanes within a cemetery,
a corner quartered, a cardinal quad, a cross, from
above, the one star in the gloaming
bright in its area. Was that a yes? It had been
a day of winking receptivity. I looked up
the word fend to see if its stave and manage
meanings had separate derivations. Haven't.
Manage, is it, one does in the little city
of a cemetery, to stroll its arbors
completely and return to the gates?
Come to know its mounds and overhang
shag semantics and compare
what cannot be known of shade
and piano stone and serenity in
the rest of Boston. Sat right here with
a feuilleton once, wet and dry in the rain
reading, happy to feel on the page
an every now and then thump of life
and keep the thread of the narrative.
Fend is only short for defend, of course,
whereas I had expected a fennel frond
or a foil or something inner forest feeling.
Who meant it first as doing without others
who might have helped? Jackson, Thomas.
1627, in his Treatise of the Divine Essence
and Attributes: they do not direct their brood

in their motions but leave them to fend
for themselves. Not far in you find
a place from which to view the broken
families, on the knitted moss and natural
gravel beneath the juniper and fir.
I wonder who they were.

Pterygium

Hallmark meteorology: a little what-if weather
sworn over time to the ridgeline conditions
the basiners downvalley to the lucky look
of trouble. In an updraft apprehension
replenishes the cloud, a steady sort of borrowing

against promise. Welling at bottom, a slow spring fills
centrally where it plummets, a sump and font that fills

convexity out to its inky meniscus, whether
there the landmark melancholy were owing
to the mirror it lends the blotted sky or to the condition
of abysses. A cygnet is drawn anyway, milky, apprehensive,

to water's edge, to study his launch, and fixes his look
across the curvature, a creature whose rarity may—look

again—enrapture each round-turning drake that fills
brown the pond beyond his brink.

                              One's apprehensive
approach can be determinative: not even to ask outright whether,
of his irregularity, it were wound or condition,

as though on the surface sensitive material were issuing
from the trademark metonymy, a little wing

a pilot polishes on his boy's lapel. His broken look,
portioned out, is symptomatic, a precondition
even, of the miscue an infatuated lover ever fills
his windy pennant with, predicative of what-if weather.

What if you could see from your signature? A preemptive
brokerage, like a birthright, but more comprehensive

since the undersigned self-attests, and winks the other, undergoing
the immediate future: I'm with damage, the weather—
what of it?—a blown impunity. Who holds this look
holds a man. Did it hurt? Was he smitten? Did it fill

when he was in velvet with shorthorn, and condition
him to devilshine? Was it mothered? Is its nacre a condition

thereof? Or is the birthmark masonry? Or perhaps if
we "drag it clear from its glacial stagnation" it fulfills
what Baudelaire proposed was beauty. Misfortune
exteriorized, rescuing liquidity from the mint. Now look

through that. Now see through these. The weather,
refocusing this way, is a matter to do (the matter either

weeping over) less with conditions than with outlook,
in the pink or, near squint, in the given umbrage
one from another has taken to bed—

$\qquad\qquad\qquad\qquad$ where partiality refills.

Edge of Water, Portage Bay, Washington

Standalone heron borrowing a pylon in Portage Bay
       accounts payable
according in quarter turns her head by the dial
of her beak to motion under current
                      until certain. One of seven.

But the night began later.
Even after the soaring bridge hid
the assignation, the dark water passing darker
through. A grade higher, inland, on the return path
the tedium of midges lifted that hung about
kissing level.

Like we left the guild victorious.

Eclogue in Line to View *The Clock* by Christian Marclay

Okay, but now imagine someone,
one of fifty, say, in the queue, fiftieth first
and advancing little, somewhere within
the seventy-two-hour window of efficacy
for post-exposure prophylaxis, and, later,
in the screening room watching *The Clock*
with the few dozen others in rows behind and ahead
who had waited too. He knows he has to
but he hasn't yet. We pick it up there.
It is two thousand eleven a few more days.
The movie tells what time it is.
In poetry too we all face forward.

The History of Ideas, 1973–2012

Here we are all, by day; by night we're hurl'd,
by dreams, each one, into a several world.

—Robert Herrick

Alienation

*In the different forms of alienation some other entity had obtained what
was proper to man: in religion it was God, in politics the State,
in economics the market process and cash nexus*

At the end of the capriccio we each reinvented the last night
of youth as we knew it, in which,

                         so you wait, one determines,
    there are no prerogatives but to return to the car
and fog up the windows with your socked feet and sulking.
        If the old compunction in your mouth will not now
      be voided, and you won't outlast righteousness, seal in
the soda sound of your breathing, and then open the door again
      on night, moonless more profitably, as to walk off here
        from the commonplace porchlight has the benefit of peril.

      Or, in her bed that night have the protagonist ask, Is what I am
    the thing I can do? All her life, one determines, she will mean
        never to forget the vocation's imperative, as the finer dancer
          remembers falling
                is better than fashioning a fall.

   First, my body related me to others whom I did not choose,
and this was before I was a subject, so what I am comprises that
      humiliation of my judgment in matters of love and this
    attempt to recover ecstasy, volunteer for pleasure. At least

match waists with Evan. Rotate the trunk while holding
    the arms fixed in a hoop shape. Polish your elbow. Zero in
on sympathetic laddering. Follow anyone's finger.

Maybe at the end
head out into the movement field a final time
with the company and the touchpoint actions
a sideline of proctors listed to see you repeat. Select
pleasures made tasks, let my body find
what to do   besides, please, because
this familiarity is the one I leave with.

Or, in the corner of the boat the tide turns beneath
a spider covers her territory. Tomorrow, the long day's
sun. And you are he who carries her eggs in his hair and needs
his something slaked. Him in the mirror tarnishing above
the stoppered bottles. In that bay beyond the bayside
bar—around whose cool brass rail a boy disunites his
heel and sandal—she runs again the rim of the rest of time.
Since, why stop at youth, one determines.

On your stomach, rear back high. Yes, this is my well
you've fallen in, and I need you now to remove your shirt.
The fire moss is crawling with why you came, and say that
in Portuguese, and again looking now into the camera
say it. Boa noite. Boa noite, Vitor. Come out from among
the others and be ye separate. Starmint stuck in a dish of pennies.

Or, you teach the child to spell his name in sparkler light and feel
you shouldn't've. He autographs the night, but it's not hereditary.
Light another.

So who are we? We are the life force power of the universe,
with manual dexterity and two cognitive minds

Authority

*Where the correlative of reason was conviction and where the correlative
of power was obedience, the correlative of authority was trust*

Your job—she gives another to the child
hip-high—is to heat the money in your hands
to the optimum warmth for purchase. Cagey,
the diversion in the same coin as his want.
It buys her time, enough that once
they round the corner, she might break into a sprint,
as one might with a pet who can keep up. But
the prophet makes eyes in his open fists
of the nickels' glint, and we see he forbears
our guess her hector gets lost in the flash

when as if by swale we all give way to expel
a customer from the clench of us without her.
For what beneath the moths who have all night
to live do we brace ourselves as we approach?
We lean to find again the boy's outguess of us.

Demand is double at the walk-up window, where
punishment for paltry want is to tell it again
into plexiglass the color of slobber, so others
in the bleach of halogen light may deal
their disparagement forward. For what if not
dishonor are we braced, rehearsing what to ask?
Repetition is a machine, a machine
for converting request into appeal; and
commerce, then, the window's byproduct or
balm, depending. Red hot cashews, yellow bag.

Only because we visit by day do we know
at night what to call at the walk-up window
where two aisles of open merchandise end at
the sacral plates of clerks before us who, if
on pulleys they were carts instead or vending claws,
would be by now concussed and dented by
lever malevolence outright.
                          The prophet stands eye level
with the vending plunge, a here and now mechanism
he would need to invent to operate, and stands
between it and his mother. Yellow bag.

Because there is not enough money in the world, people steal;...
because there is not enough recognition, they make art

Casuistry

Moral solutions to moral problems, so "situational ethics" pleaded, must spring from the
unrepeatable decisions of unrepeatable personalities in unrepeatable situations

It scarcely varies. You make a knot amateur and complex
and ask someone over to soak it and, before he leaves,
you pull it tighter than you might otherwise alone and
dry entirely, and then wait for disintegration, you wait
longer than you live, this way. Only then acknowledge
the mess of tether or lariat was never tied to you.

So help me, yes. Since I was last contrite, I trailed attrition
for reasons other than love, if that be the measure, sorrier
still. The sleeping kittens are evenly spaced, in print,
and in quandary the canny dogs stationary each page
of paper towel fewer, tighter around the furry tube.
Court is not going to adjourn itself your leniency.

Each table elected a secretary and every scritch
beneath the vestments under pretense of deliberation
has entered the record, a tell to decode. Curl
and arch, everything about you assents except your say.

Read that last bit back to me.
                              Depends on how you mean
orientation. Is it admissible I brought it from boyhood,
which beat to poetry a path, to stand and petition frankly
even then anything in no way arbitrative, a blackberry bush,

or an organ pipe nest of dauber bees, pumping subsequence
for consequence. All the woodpiles I ever visited
in the godfearing missions were ricked between two trees
prised apart and proctoring their dead. I'd watch
that wimpled tarpaulin cagily and take my answer inside.

There was a clearing deeper in where two cousins could
do it together, call it company coming over, practice
a neatening routine, keeping sunlight even and sculptural,
planting branches and bundling needles before—they're here—
the shadow enters the ring. Breezily, the guest was
enormity of night. From there on in, the girl and boy grow
complicit in a switch and reverse preparations, to leave.
You're much too kind a host, it's awfully late however.

    Permit me, I am older than your complacency
who may not have scouted out the position yet
you send me in, to ask, and explain asking
what comes next to mean something forever. Surely
in chambers you have noted man and office split, loyalties
divide. That too is the self-situation game, propitious
pausing here and singing please, and can be by decree a career.

One hand where the gown gathers, a substitute sensation,
some room drape-drawn around the privacy of your purchase.
It scarcely varies. You rush the genteel institution for the redress
you seek, fill up the institute with near space and chittering

at the underwear drawer. A little pecan somewhere
around the band, but sweeter. This is data Justice needs,
data that will erode. Still. At bottom under cover of night
another covering, the mattress ticking.

                           And then?

Your honor: Yes. Read that last bit back to me.

A pigeon is someone who comes along just in time to keep her sponsor sober

Education

What Heidi's grandfather learned from the eagle he taught himself

Aggregate is a pavement rough on the feet. We spread it around
the allotment gardens, where monuments are most prone.
At level grade, we introduce the churn, a procedural masonry
flocked with beak and shell and pattern after, a deuteronomy
all over the ground, much like that the maestri spotted
on the monticule and derived, halfway down again,
of starshower.
　　　　　　Trueness to type is the objective in aggregate,
and chalking it up, roughly, the signature business
of our internal audit, summarized over the translator before
the hearings of grievance. In truth the gardeners
are lucky to have us, and if their gratitude is tactical
it is no less affecting to have pressed into our aprons
the gentians indigenous to First Elevation.

A blossom sometimes, in their parlance, volunteers
out of season, and it is not without precedent we
element the youth we find one morning at the pour
and pattern after. It seems an act of love paradoxically,
the expulsion they call going to seed—his kiss curl twisted
up and out in a manner we now recognize as preparatory,
fontwater wet. While we work his boredom brings to him
one of our handtrucks and a duet all day to choreograph,
rock-tip-twisting into dervish a leverage of himself until
the beck he was assigned to search our faces for
escapes him and we break silence. He yanks his balance,
wheels out, skids again. When we escort the probate

to the audition granted him and his hum among us
in the melody of the closing prayer the novitiates lead
after grievances is resonant in our walk back, we notice
like nuns the march of our feet in its beat and stagger,

whereupon in testiness we huff and ditch the stiffened
batch, then mellow. We clap out dust from the proving trays.

Extraordinary achievement is less about talent than it is about opportunity

Empathy

The insistence by some that the distinguishing characteristic of empathy
is the merging of subject and object has not seemed by others
to be the important requirement

The rip in the piedmont came with a flue inherent.
The scent everyone said was mephitic, but we stayed.
From beyond its sediment apron, it was not an eye at all.
In the negatives it looks like fire, with hair of light above.
It's being weird, everyone says, looking down.
We're not boring holes, we're facilitating flues.

In software development, you begin by creating
a persona, someone whose problems are yours
to understand. We knew a few things about
the cinder aroma. In sandstone a sink is customary,
and is equally likely under water. Under water,
it is often called a hole. Blue Hole, locals say.
It may be colder there if you're swimming across.
The water that gets in the rip is rain and won't amount.
Remember Marianne Moore looked into a grave
with a man, and her mother oversaw: it was ocean.
The rip too is the kind of hole that gets not full but
fraught.
            He has a problem with his eye, the pit of it
moves around. He keeps his voice in his throat,
you can feel it. Say it, sky. The sky might, that's
the sound he makes, fricative, glottal plosive, moan.

Disproven: the illusion things gather at the rip.
We can assume q is why we slept poorly near,

especial but why. We can assign its isolation
to the beta version and run a trial. As green
can sometimes pick up green around, or a geyser sigh.

Whose counsel precedes him is always home.   I awoke
compelled to wash it once; the wolves had been so rough.
We came to call the night watch a sight bath,
mooning in, because, I suppose, of the way
one acclimates. Now play the same melody next
to a sink in the earth; here and there, ambient echolalia, like
a little genius interpreting reprimand.

The telephoto footage has not yet surfaced, and I
grow anxious. No results for "volcano goes bankrupt."
The clop of alpaca on the butte once drifted in
on the wind.
                  It's true we presuppose him a user, false
his facelessness is sacrosanct, set apart from fantasy.
We voted the crank down by a narrow majority.
On our elbows, we worked on that imitation some,
after Moore. The sensor had a housing and, well,
we inventory everything. When we reorganized camp
to make of the tents a floor-through, we'd wanted
to sympathize, to think of thinking without branching.

Whose brand is famous descends within. Everybody knows
who was deceived by revenant Nobody and personnel.
The story is worn. But to look one-eyed at something
was how our photography changed our painting; lament
via epistemology.

Climb to where the tarn is a coin
in size and shine and feel a final time the bossing
of your own lost pocket change. At your feet should be
the red shale calcite with which to rubricate
back at the rip, and turn the questions down.

What part of me goes over when I imagine the chalk drop?
Is it by virtue of being more mineral more planetary below?
From now on in, a blanket fallibilism as far as it will go.
Whose motive we know is measurable conforms.
Wool in the air a kind of krill for the whale of the hole.

We are not a self-starting institution here, we only disapprove
of something when somebody asks us to

Motif

Until the nineteenth century Englishmen habitually spoke of acting on a motive
rather than acting from a motive

No sooner, like the frame, had landscape
on its own a *raison d'etre* than arose the demand it be
a verb. Capability Brown was a rented talent, eight stone and six,
and satisfied a clientele with expanse to an extent,
and strode a property remarking motif in the middle distance.
It's as though he pinches from the very soil
the pause, they appraised, given in the visit. Inside,
       his lifespan measured more or less the change:
       the withdrawing room become the drawing room.

      On hunches on haunches they let us know
they are cautious acting, the bestiary we overturned
on the ground we had meantime made a rink. This one's
early on in the series, see the pronghorn's consternation.
Speech bubble in the clearing all caps why bereave uncertainty of hope.
No repealing *raison d'etre*, comrade. Umbrage,
                        foreshadow. Here's us
      overseeing the meadow's potential,
nothing left of the locative, nothing locomotive
to mirror our thoughts: Less way wending
and more windswept coif and vector, we say, more
push off at the wall. I saw he wore a tear-away smock
and scheduled a second studio visit.

Scumble a stretch of unprimed Turkish cotton duck and already
the back of the painting is not the back of the canvas.

Roll your eyes if this checks out. For a living, if.
There is another city, called Is,
eight days' journey from Babylon. This one
was going to have at the end of a road a round
of wild turkeys jumping in some tangled wire. When I say it back
the sign reads nothing repeats Pennsylvania like liberty.

Up in the corner, a terrapin falters five more inches along the perimeter
before pedaling again the earthen berm.

What's unique about language is that the creatures
that develop it are highly vulnerable to being eaten

Mountains and Hills, Literary Attitudes Toward

On the question of mountain origin and the place of hills in the scheme
of things the two greatest reformation thinkers stood opposed

The towpath put them gradual against the mountain habit,
so any disinclination visible from camp was in the scheme
drawn over the swinging bean kettle—at bottom he'd reprieve
Luther the more moonshone work of sleeping openly with
what he tends. The tradeback of assignments was
left an option and it was option that made a man behaviorally
lovely like Luther. He liked rather to say of the sheep winter
it was more minding than tending. How is it we found
ourselves here, he might ask, ever and again, our dotty flock
picking out the sun like lettering well before, in place of hills,
there was the word. Here the flap is like a rollback screen,
he tells his dream to clear it for another, meter reading aloud
the light and, what little room they have, his inward turn shows
what shepherding is, holding Calvin hard against his grace.
Pull the plate.

Worry is the misuse of imagination

Paradox

It is not surprising that suicide, or individual self-cancellation, self-annihilation,
became a recurrent topic of paradox:

We came to, raced past, and let stand a syllogism
and doubled back, which is already metaphorical, I began,
by way of example. To explain what we ran Overnight
on, though it should not have been incumbent on us
to establish that a platform any more is soft-,
not hardware, commonly, it needed to be premissed
that sleep and dream are not as wood and ivy.

      At the foot of the bed like the crawl of other news
I saw my chart move. Read: a relief of duty
had elicited new liege, to which the brief and I
were something subject, a critical biography. It made
its leathery clap, as of old wattage spooling
inside the helmet of a meter a reader records
at her interval. A workstudy at the humming post
delays: a moment effervesces in the sound well
roaring beneath the rapids where swiftness was. Atop,
the little boat turning still in the eddy.
                        An hysteria there,
a sloppy recrimination, contempt stirring devotion, someone
calling an apology into the water. It sinks through,
why such recollection is overcome. I note in the crawl,
This is the shore of the worst thing possible. The rest
of his days like a puff of shale are dispersal of the dustup.

What is the word for a stack of stones used as a marker?
I erased all other texts in my handheld, so that this one

would ever be the oldest, the bottommost. Not pylon, not
mignon, not riprap at switchbacks, commoner to the grave.
Siste viator. I got here as fast as I could.

Plainly the ticker evidenced that
somesthesia could be retrained, shift by shift, and pinpointed
the extrapolation by which we had imported hence
the weakest cause for closing out of Distant Emil:
even a bath is a banishment provided it tops the ears.

Past pertinence we could not hear the rain of reason
in this business about whether—in pressing record rather
than signaling help—we saved the wrong thing.

Character is both developed and revealed by tests, and all of life is a test

Space

At night only our own sun is turned away from us, but all the other
suns (that is, fixed stars) of the universe shine upon us as by daytime

In the happy outparish of the late American afternoon, in the Tyra hour
the scholia on ownership recount but deprave
the premises. Here when we nod we nod at a slant
I nearly insist anyone concede, but a scold among followers
soon gallops the savannah with the other once voluble qualms:
once within us an axis rose upright with reason,
as we long knew from lockstep shadow.
      I walk still with the party but it discountenances me.

      The beings were built a precept, maximizing, Own It.
And the renaissance of daytime accustomed us at home provisionally
at first to formulate the lesson: let it belong to you, where *it* is anything
suffered and survived, where belonging, if anything,
turned our sofa sectionals at the caesura
open-elbow to mirror mother's; there we found
opprobrium a birthright reversible,
                  and we honeyed assent ourselves.
As if by prophecy, the daughter avatar is drawn easily, like the last
of box tissue, the stake whereto we tied enlightenment and from that pyre
the pep—now as the maxim glosses: indicate ownership.

      Cede the ruin read the note
monarch to nomarch I'd carried for days
and brought the answer I carry home: my own errand arm
blackened with a putrid paste. Downriver overnight
on the cedar barge it began to sting
            and the coarse buccaneer

whose charge I was permitted me immersion in the wake,
mean relief—indeed, quicker agony—but cool.

For the first time I dreaded the coming sun,
knowing what insult to the pharaoh I bring in my repatriation,
and made my wish in the water worsen for reaches beneath.

If you don't visit a bad neighborhood, the bad neighborhood will visit you

Symmetry

Whenever a form or unit of life comes into being on any spot of the universe then any such occurrence, taken by itself, runs counter to the general trend towards an increase of the entropy

By what shade stain was left we told
aptitude, and woke him, at last. Where prior elders
may have swabbed with resin and covered properly as he lay
the birthday boy with falcon down
we borrow from the annals only the prior elder prayer.

     Not that he'd remember. We couldn't
get the recitation solemn enough. Worse, the huddle,
more worrisome when legislative, is men's agreement going in
to raise temerity from downcast scrutiny.
Piteous the metal taste of smoking and crying. Bereft
the transactive sacrament. Until the lashes flutter.

Saw him later in the same puny dyad we'd all had,
rocking the subdivision no one in the rumbleseat 'sides his baby.
Down Alvernon, we dressed the tracking shot to dolly with
his figure against the Tyvek homewrap, should he turn.

It's my experience the event gets less eccentric, not more,
becoming plainly a circle, by the end, like the soil spot
you tell ripeness by. A tart disclosure asks that you blush back
if you're going to stay for the drop.
              Like an illness welling,
awaiting him, it came upon me to redraw our crest,
to entwine the filigree, tie compunction about belief:

the bird on the cadge sorting

through its bib in a final ministration, as if undoing the torse. Grant,

to be born and live as variously as possible. Unless
this takes, whereby togetherness, our given and ground,
would lift or even belie the law, it intermits the trend:
alone is always alone again. Grant, we turn you down.

If you lived here, you'd be home by now

Time

Mathematical continuity (i.e., infinite divisibility) belongs only to the spatial segment by which duration is inadequately symbolized, not to duration itself

I stayed in on Island Day, all my wreaths banging
the hut in the wind. What discipline
has to do with it disinclination
modulates, one kettle testy moment to the next
a personal sorcery. So high I nested in abasement
decisions ceremoniously to have none of
the erstwhile custom custom has it we observe
to uncup an islander's espadrilles from her heels
and dance on the furry planks down at the Jetty.

Or, when the famous blimp emerges from the treeline
and heaves easily to its mark and airdries the town
tournament from above, there's no other way but slowly,
separately, virtually, inferring what day it is, to appreciate
experience is common. What day, that is, of the year.

I lived there because people in great number are
made of time, and so event in the civitas is human.
I put myself into play, the civitas saw, to precipitate
Fleet Week, Ash Wednesday, and other
all-boats-rise public turnings of the year,
circulating the tender index I was of regularity.

Here the tidings other people are
I bring myself, myself a periodical, and refresh
the herald homepage frequently remind me why.
I bring myself around.

I let you in on Island Day, you who sat scout on the patio
and hadn't asked. Now tell me how came you to make the news.
Well as you know from the founders' day colloquium
the pioneer question was, hiding place or resting place?
Next to pinnacle I had: something to live down.
Apparently they discourage the term arriviste.

It was a funny retreat, a climb in any direction,
and I went back desultorily, as anyone does
whose only engagement is distant, to meet friends Friday
at Cliff's Edge, whose profession until then is silhouette.

Was that when you saw him, his quiver likewise heavy?
The nightlong reaching back archer and archer
upshot.

            My nightmare was a little film about death.
In an icy ground, because they receded in series or because
their torn plastic had faded, five small orange flags brought on
a memorial mood. They waved in the lowest wind. I'm sorry
it woke you. Something along the line of public works,
an old initiative, in a wash-the-faucet sort of oversight
no one yet having acted on these wicket indications.

                    When the world is flat, geopolitics means the interaction between
                                old time urges and just in time delivery

Ut Pictura Poesis

As with a colonnade, repetition not only moves through space itself
but, for the viewer, exists in time

The Fortinbras in one is the avenger we follow
in another. Foliage, way out a while back, and wet
still, low boughs. His horse noses through, eyes the size
of plums, and so soon. How was that supposed to sound,
overheard, until overcome? like a poem in which ambush
I crouch, if rooting around for wide new leaves it is I, or fern
the forest floor in patchy opportunity.
                                        The fern
in each new iteration reads the scheme, and like lace
paper pulled, overland portage fits to screen, offering hitherto
itineraries artless except for the way the mind swaps roundabout
for reconnaissant. And reverts. He wears his toque feather
above the opposite ear! we swore in the gay bar
on the gameboard of his likeness, running up
the score on whomever had been high. First sign
we saw, at the image ridge. Or at least it used to be a gay bar.

Where eventually we would decide to merge forward-dawning
with mission creep to condition horizon, which we lost
in a portmanteau, anachronism still
scales this map with vetch at the edges, in an arch,
which gives the open glade an aspect of stage
so that, and so on, the vixen might trot to her moonlit mark

mouthing the tar compound of recent kill, or

an advance man unpack his bag. This is who

we intercept, that's the play. We wait for the sun to rezone.

With the rise of the web, poetry has met its photography

NOTE

Epigraphs are excerpts from *The Dictionary of the History of Ideas*, edited by Philip Wiener, Isaiah Berlin, and George Boas, published by Charles Scribner's Sons, in 1973.

Italicized quotations at the ends of poems belong to the years 2008-2012 and may be attributed to the following epistemological body.

[seated, left to right]

Justice Jill Bolte Taylor
Justice Adam Kirsch
Justice Alcoholics Anonymous
Justice Malcolm Gladwell
Justice Antonin Scalia

[standing]

Justice Temple Grandin
Justice Human Givens
Justice Pastor Rick Warren
Justice Thomas Friedman (term extension)
Justice Chuck Palahniuk
Justice Kenny Goldsmith

Lifespan Addenda

Auspex in hospice, each of us,
home forsworn, should hope to be
visited again. Three birds
       come back, crisis apparition or
provident delivery, searching the air
in a reverie you might announce
and they'd grant you that, or I,
present for astonishment
purposes in moments
everything reset.
             The way
Guy Davenport said a bird'd be,
an attachment, mailer-daemon
returning for review ones that rook,
a parliament gathering singly.

       The grackle above the backlot
xeriscape, two feet levitated
for his mate, Pima County, el milagro,
Arizona. A casino gush
of nonpareil, openly winning
a minute long. All that ultra black
to undo his lover did. Nature spent
a fortune one day into night
I got it right. The colors trail, trail
away. The Christ Event obviating
adverbs, as it were. Not even once, not
finally. Back when I had everything

to want. The bird jumping into the hold
in the air. Attached to whatever
time is attached to.

Where for a stretch coming off
the bridge to the barrier island
the causeway veins the isthmus entirely
the stone crabs cross the street,
and gravid must, for less brackish
hatch, and a turkey buzzard
gets the picture. Never been eyed,
not that way, since, seed sown in.
The midpoint of my life, now
you see. Interruptions
across and the causeway too.
Here I am breaking the horizon.
Something unwinding still
in the car, slowing another
half mile before the turnout came
and antidote in doubleback.
Causeway transposition: from
yanking the wet sweet back body out
of the cracked case, a pause, her
fearsome red rule to return through.

The suffusion of a rich old woods'
last new growth: Election Day ferns
capitalize on shred light, an Idaho

of understory greener than spring.
Like this, the footfalls far from home
his and mine and his and mine and now
again the dotty canopy and the sink
sensation focus upward sends.
When did the world start so
the ghost berry bush by dark
is a grown down constellation,
and the newt in his hand wasabi?
The void chasing the ample rush,
heart-level, like a drawer receding
into the mountainside,
heavily the pheasant
pushes her flight deeper in.

Superfund

If this was all the access you had
to sky, looking down through
boardwalk boards into a tributary
glinting, if this was all the time
your calling or had been all
this time, and you found it, found
yourself arrested above an opening,
if purgatory were as real as bridges,
where would your religion build,
in the soft parabola of carriage
and suds, or in the hip points
your heaviness keeps in counsel
with the planks. The mill of
spiderlight and curtainwork in one
run over the impress of
cofferdam in the other. This river
in the days left to live, in
the leftover days reclamation
balances, trains its instrument
on a prospect romantic, pushy and
plainly. The joinery of the boards
is thoughtful, or the prison wish is
a watchwork through and through:
to guess at the rare punt
of a single stick's bark odyssey, or
to separate from the rummage

each drifted glyph of superscript
and gloss the passage. Drawn through
the bothway of the ribs:
a breath, and then another.
No prior experience knock wood.
Not purgatory, but overage.

The Inversion

For a while the hotboxing boys five to a car
watch parkour update the dugout
for Armageddon center of town.
Preparatory school
kids they used to know
remade.   Redistribution of mascules
      in the concentrated ecosystem, mostly
      psychomotor agitation and covering remark,
      still squinting, a backseat metric:
            dugout the length of a wiper blade.
   So the freerunners vanish
under the floodlights, which flash on
and spread over the glaucous outfield
like mystique. That was one day.

Through the truckstop fudge of mascara,
threat or ecstasy having subsided, through
either diner window, time
to decide, while he's in the men's,
      the dead, tall tangle of mallow in cheat grass
      and common tansy
      barely stirs in the opposite lot,
            and beyond, farther still from the overpass
            the steer like gurus
            move despair around.

      What else. The river doing its one
downtown contour, according to plan.
      Upstream someone has stacked antlers:
            a ruined empire's diadems. Clinting.

In early 2010 young Thomas went into
self-storage. The author bio
writes itself.   Uncle Poet other side of town
                catches a lift from a flower truck.

Made this shaky video of loose change
in a dugout. A plastic bag crosses the road
on its handles. *But that's extortion*
                a television exclaims.

Somehow it superintends,
the inversion layer, without lodestar
or sun or moon or anything we'd say
werc supervisory.
                Only each other to count
on seeing, in the pervasive velum light we have
all day. An afterlife light.

It is positional, to be under the inversion,
prepositional, undergoing it. Such is the sentence.
The situation is plain convection deficit
above ground. No breeze,
        warm or wet, no breakthrough of influx.
                We push around the word until,
                and lug the other since.
        It isn't balance, it's double work, we hail
            still in our own air, incorporated.
Careful as abatement.

Smalltown Lift

One last stop, he says. And they drive to Westside Lanes.
I grew up bowling. I don't want to bowl. It was raining.
We're not going to bowl, the circus carpet dark with gum
beneath them, and he parts the curtains on the best
photo booth in town. He feeds it the three dollars, Get
in. They somehow share the short ridged stool. In here
we have to tell one another one true thing. *You first.* Click.
This is the best way I could think to have my arm around you.
Click. Click. Click.

Sonnets in Diaghilev's Beard

1.

Before bed in the hotel a boy shot his brother
on cable, prising apart the fence wire in
the opening frames. That I reconstruct it
by heart, or must, is a bafflement, a pleasure
for Diaghilev who cleans his beard like a bird
in the dust of my fund. He feeds and sleeps on me
although the swing of pail and twitch of rifle in
my shoulders, suppressed, builds symphonic
and plays all night so rest awaits the performance
caught in barbs, a morning accident my sum
discharges. I unmemorize it. And when then I run
the bath in the deluxe water closet I bathe
instead in chicory and cocoa pure from Port
au Prince. I'm working on a piece called Wattles.

2.

The tempo of the rain is a better god,
a control, like they say in sciences, the all else
equal I vary in my pulse. I pee a little
in my pants or nearly, and check effects. You know
there are quiet means to scatter and collect
oneself. In that, all others on the flight
mistake the opportunity we have in touch
and tangent. But you, as I, play who-like-me
with faces. Diaghilev will not understand
the air is made of such devotions as

ours. He hears a prattle when we ladder out
each other's language. The tempo of the rain
is less to him than wets umbrella. I held
the cane of it to my ear to listen, remember.

3.

It's popular openly to confide in Seattle,
I wasn't ready to hear it. It means experience
came later and instructed where counsel
failed. Convertible to dance in the steerage
of the shoulders, the confidence of the wrong
past oversight, then, halted, fill the pause
with a hearse of quiet, belated as a bruise.
I spend the time Diaghilev explains
local custom determining by what
agency the newsprint smudges on the score
he spanks into his open hand and leaves
on the hotel dresser become in me,
to slalom, an archipelago of keys.
The detour pennanted, the piracy.

4.

He says what passes between us is sortilege,
his word, and he thinks it unnatural, your toss
for instance of the witchhazel bough onto
the hay in our stroll. You will recognize

at Interlaken the gesture I cannot now
resist in his pantomime. As if it would ignite.
I admit I have the atlas open to environs
of my tenderness toward you, and further
I await his tracing interest in the routes
and rail. It will end in love for you, my end,
his clenching speculation turned study
over the stand, when intent positions him
like a carapace the beetle leaves, and
as my animus knows a better area.

Rods and Cones

To be built a squirrel, to scale, to be
proportional, at the side of the shortrail
track, in the wild onions, her reflex
celerity prime, each eye circuited directly to
her cortex so, unlike human vision, hers is
not coarsened by summation: that
quick is the squirrel. When she
stands, is made to stand, one foot favored,
petite and lifted, on the three others
plantigrade and looks to god, who
stands behind his handiwork, waist high,
is made to look, she sees how significant
scale is to Papa, the back of his boy's head
the size of his own cupping hand. The track
needs to pass through something, and a town
is a lot to ask, a place that can produce
a people, enough of a people that one
in a platform dozen can be a passerby.
I-35 overpass suggestion: Kansas City.
Slow turns around coarsening, around
summation, why can't I react sooner
to what I see? (The boy pivots around
his crown his paper visor). Took me a minute
to replace my comb in the pocket of my
jacket. Benches to suggest time, benches
the squirrels comb the grass beneath, looking.
Benches are a fixture in Papa's plan.
Children of such a man carry his schedule

and watch for the time of arrival. In boys,
to track what's coming is to alert
the men they'll be by spotting the switch
ahead. The boy agitates at the vantage he attains
where his reverie tailors his stupor, and
the car wobbling that disturbs the primary
pit boss is the very thing he fills
his interest with, that and the tiny townie
articulation, an elbow out, elbow in
behavior. Some barrels here holding what,
nickel per bag, simulation mulch.
A squirrel, too, looks for what to see, her way
headed. A piping sheet of pink townies
immigrates on the rear cargo car
of the main line, slowing at the three-way
stub switch, son and station and he who
says so, and pulls into the infield. In form:
an innocuous midlevel executive
having a sandwich, a girls basketball coach
covering cross-handed his boner, a car
wobbling quality control specialist battering
a tie, everybody still on the vine.
Coverall Papa himself crawls under
the reality skirt to the primal yard to
snip them, fit his jewelling monocle, rods
and cones magnetic, and mix the liquid acrylics.

Littlest Illeity

Always there is agency, cleverer
the decree holding an instrument at
the moment it sounds. Belgrade
baby rattle that might spill if baby
tried. Otherwise a pacifier. No I do
enjoy being made to wonder. John
always has a jar, this one, too, large
enough to contain much more
solution than it does. Its settlement
capacity is deep, shallow albeit.
Is water a solution? Was anything
chemical happening when he
made the sound in the jar sound?
Seemed he was interested instead
in showing it, until I chimed in.
The swill of it, holy water from
the sound. Inside the wash were
people—no one you know—people
forms, the sort at whom a tinker toils,
no taller than an ornery thumbnail,
and daubs a cornflower matte cap on,
in a workshop the favorite nephew
and his boy friend know. Why
are people forms waiting for a train
to pass them ever over settled in
the meanwhile of a water jar
even John may not know.

Before I ask I tell him why.
I like that sound. I pressed record
in my heart when he stirred it
once again soliciting the sound.
A fifth click you can't pick out.
Is brahm a unit of measurement
is the kind of thing I think, and
John is the friend I have who
entertains it. Little unpainted people
forms, fixities in a stroll, remains
already, instrumental once in a
while of water, weird, for the tink
on glass the plastic go-round pisses.
He doesn't have to explain it.

Brownie's Motel Plus

The sexual career was said to begin when I was hired,
a doffing hat on a pair of Albuquerque boots or else
would have my application returned unread, but so long
have I been an inveterate holder of ladders, his and higher, gutter
huggers, I know angles and give in the ground, I know
footed flip locks and anticipation coming and going backward
down. These were the right words: wait two minutes
and follow me in. Doable. I better the threshold, even crossing
thinking on my feet with caviling the nightshift,
a reverse frost, an inside wipe. If anything
we smelled for all the world alike, that was
the prank of it. We made love what no one wondered
at the greeting desks about. We backed up how we needed,
we brought our heavy unretractable concatenations with us, enormously
silent, into narrow ten pm breezeways, maneuvering among
the kiosks, a pair of lockstep skis which will not park, unbent,
and turned the pages of their papery magazines. With these
we said, it rung when we said,
I think I've found my building blocks. I know how now.
I am a sentence closer; hence, what part in my show do you want:
hold the ladder or brave it in the air? Give me
pull through like we saw in the repagination,
rivers of text reallocating, an arroyo caution-placarded
for the oncoming gush through fossil wash.
It just rung, and the guy—when I turned to see the delay alight
on you—was wise to the prank of it, and sent me off alone
to twenty six, with, on its flat red plastic tongue, the key to try.

And By and By

A second bird somewhere he said undid the doom,
but I never saw either. On we walked. Women feel
intimate face to face. Men, shoulder to shoulder,
I read later in his notes, without citation.

Eclogue Through the Night

What one person would I put on board to hoist me up if leitmotif
and timing were hastening on and worsening my rural depot outpost past,
snowpatches in the ditch still, the fathered bootlaced boy in Wyeth worried,
and clamber when our arms had locked his steady leverage up to where he'd
braced himself smart against the prow of palettes, his velocity constant and
his interest piqued in rescue of a wet new friend, you. By pearling or
by paneling, your eyes holding heaves of mine. Only, now I want to
switch. Hurry, you can make it,

                      switch. Make it reach. Are we tramping now
to Peridelphia by musculature of rail and had you known and how the payoff
of sylvan demigods was flicker light on tall blue spruce and, as luck
would have it, the gash I splash aboard with was from mirror pieces
in my pocket I carried myself by the wrist from Spokane herewith, some
low stakes modeling, then the safe passage it would buy us. This is your part,
darkness pressing in, the annotative margins and, for mine, I read through
the night. When you're ready you can tell me, if I can put the catch in late,
whose is your freight under all that breathing blanket. I'll sleep. Keep reading.

Edge of Water, Moiese, Montana

Just this dry mix
of whitening pink and mauve and blue bean
powdered over cache, which becomes beneath
the least lick of the Jocko River
market radish red and cobalt, and some stand
half in bath—
               To outlast alone the doubt one is alone, or
acclimate to a decency, differ in temperature
from the big and little stones in the scree decreasingly,
and search for a place to build a spine.

The phrase for it, catch myself, is fugitive
even. About Moiese the dry first fact
of a scarab, a white one specked in the chalk rock
whose antennae, nearly fabric, are data-fond
and then the woozy look again downriver
an hour on: moose maybe, opposite
and large enough, a legend at the water table
filling the green shade brown. Too, about
Moiese, to spot her, or anything, is a decision.

Put that third. Make a rule. Edges of water
are promise places. Lie back bare and
there is a cable pulling your next thought
to the sun. Rake your face cheek to jaw
with broken mica, and the moth traffic
triples at your back. Is that a fact?

Notes & Acknowledgments

"The City State" and "According to Herodotus" are part of a larger untitled project with poems by Richard Siken. The full collaboration was published in *Likestarlings* in 2012.

"Which of These Alberts" aligns with and borrows from scenes in Frederick Wiseman's 1985 documentary, *Racetrack*.

In "Eclogue of Sig Alert on the Ten East" phrases are appropriated from the "text paintings" of Los Angeles artist Larry Johnson. Many of these can be seen in the catalogue, edited by Russell Ferguson, that accompanies Johnson's 2008 Hammer Museum exhibition.

"Pferd": in memory of Francis J. Blanchfield, Jr. (1945–2013).

"Pterygium" is for Doug Stockstill.

From *The History of Ideas, 1973–2012*, in "Alienation" the phrases "my body related me to others whom I did not choose" and "humiliation of…my judgment in matters of love" are borrowed from Judith Butler's *Precarious Life*.

From *The History of Ideas, 1973–2012*, "Paradox": in memory of Rodney Jack, and with thanks to Wayne Johns.

////

Some of these poems were first published in magazines. My gratitude to the editors.

1110: "Edge of Water, Portage Bay, Washington"
A Public Space: "*The History of Ideas, 1973–2012*: Casuistry"
The Awl: "Pferd," "Pterygium"
Boston Review: "*The History of Ideas, 1973–2012*: Paradox"
The Brooklyn Rail: "The Inversion," "Lifespan Addenda," and "Brownie's Motel Plus"
Cincinnati Review: "Thank You Mood"
Company: "Nurse Mustn't Rummage," "S Apostrophe S," "*The History of Ideas, 1973–2012*: Alienation," and "…Education."
Denver Quarterly: "*The History of Ideas, 1973–2012*: Time" and "…Authority"

Lana Turner: "*The History of Ideas, 1973–2012*: Motif," "…Ut Pictura Poesis," and
"…Mountains and Hills, Literary Attitudes Toward"
Like Starlings: "The City State" and "According to Herodotus"
Maggy: "Edge of Water, Nimrod Falls, Montana,"; "Eclogue in Line to View
The Clock by Christian Marclay"; *The History of Ideas, 1973–2012*: Empathy";
and "Sonnets in Diaghilev's Beard"
Manor House Quarterly: "Eclogue Onto an Idea"
Map: "Starter Garden," "Which of These Alberts"
Or: A Literary Tabloid: "*The History of Ideas, 1973–2012*: Space" and "…Symmetry"
The Nation: "Superfund"
The Paris Review: "Smalltown Lift"
PEN Poetry Series: "Man Roulette," "In Their Motions," "And By and By"
Poetry International: "Paranoia Places Its Faith in Exposure"
The Poetry Project Newsletter: "Open House"
Volt: "Funny Loss of Face"; "Eclogue of Sig Alert on the Ten East"; and
"Rods and Cones"

////

The suite of poems, *The History of Ideas, 1973–2012*, was first published as a chapbook by Spork Press in 2013. Thanks to Richard Siken and Drew Burk.

////

This book is for John Myers, to whom I attune.

Minuets, exeunts, skinnies, diaghilevs, declaratives, scrolls, inventories, letting cups, suet cake, and stations: you make poetry run along life again.

110

////

To Karen Brennan, Mary Jane Nealon, Cal Bedient, Chris Nealon, Eileen Myles, Boyer Rickel, Richard Siken, Jason Zuzga, Sandra Alcosser, Merrill Gilfillan, Maggie Nelson, Jacqueline Waters, Rodney Phillips, Samuel Ace, TC Tolbert, Michael Hansen, Thomas Macfie, Annie Guthrie, Matthew Burgess, Daniel Nohejl, Lou Pepe, Jesse Aron Green, and Emery Jones: thank you for each exchange that built, rebuilt, and improved this book.

This book took shape in the supportive, immersive community and valley landscape of Missoula, Montana. I am deeply grateful for my friends, students, and colleagues there.

Special thanks to Amy Plumb Oppenheim for her permission to use on this book's cover an image from Dennis Oppenheim's 1977 installation in Missoula, "Wishing the Mountains Madness."

Finally, great thanks to Stephen Motika for his expertise, his conviction, and his many efforts, and to Margaret Tedesco and to everyone at Nightboat whose artistry and knowhow were essential.

NIGHTBOAT BOOKS

Nightboat Books, a nonprofit organization, seeks to develop
audiences for writers whose work resists convention and transcends
boundaries. We publish books rich with poignancy, intelligence,
and risk. Please visit our website, www.nightboat.org, to learn
about our titles and how you can support our future publications.

The following individuals have supported the publication of this
book. We thank them for their generosity and commitment to the
mission of Nightboat Books:

Kazim Ali
Elizabeth Motika
Benjamin Taylor

This book was made possible by grants from The Fund for Poetry
and the New York State Council on the Arts Literature Program.

NYSCA